Jonah
A Whale of a Tale

John Ryan

A LION PICTURE STORY
Oxford · Batavia · Sydney

Long ago in a far-off country, three people were fishing on a river bank.

"Look, Uncle! I've caught another," Dan cried excitedly, giving the fish to the old man beside him. "That's the third today... just right for our supper!"

"I always feel sorry for the fish," said Rachel. "It can't be much fun being caught."

"It's the worm on the hook I'm sorry for," said the old man. "It isn't much fun being swallowed, I can tell you!"

"How do you know, Uncle?" asked Dan.

"Because I *was* swallowed once... by a fish too. I'll tell you about it, if you like."

"Yes! Yes! Go on!" cried the children. "Tell us, please, Uncle Jonah!"

And so Jonah began his story...

"Well," he said, "in the country of Assyria there
was this great city called Nineveh. It was huge.
It took three days just to walk round it!

"The city was full of horrible people; selfish and wicked they were! Their ways were different from ours. Our people hated them and they hated us.

"Well, one day I was just sitting at home minding my own business, when all of a sudden God, yes, God himself, spoke to me: 'Up you get, Jonah!' he said. 'I've got a job for you.' "

"That must have been a surprise," said Dan.

"Surprise? I'll say it was. You could have knocked me down with a feather.

" 'You must go to the people of Nineveh,' God went on. 'Speak to them and tell them that if they don't mend their ways there'll be trouble. I, God, shall destroy them all, and their city too. Tell them I say so.'

"Now if God asks you to do something important it's best to do it. But I was young and foolish in those days. I thought I knew better—I wasn't going near Nineveh for anyone! The *last* thing I wanted was to save our enemies from God's anger.

"So I went down to the nearest sea-port and booked a passage on a ship going to the furthest place I could think of.

"I might have guessed it was no use! God knew exactly what I was up to. He always does. No sooner had we put to sea than the clouds gathered, the wind got up …

"… and lashed the sea into such a fury…

... that very soon we were in the middle of a terrible storm."

"Weren't you scared, Uncle?" asked Rachel.

"Well, actually," said Jonah, "I'd fallen asleep as soon as I got aboard, but the sailors were terrified.

"They all started praying to all the gods they could think of, hoping that one of them could save them from being shipwrecked and drowned.

"But it didn't do any good. The hurricane only blew harder.

"Then the captain noticed me, snoring away in my bunk. He woke me up to see if I had a god who might help us.

"Of course, I guessed just what the trouble was. It was all *my* fault for running away from the true God and not doing what he told me.

" 'You'd better throw me overboard,' I said to the captain. 'Then maybe God will stop the storm.'

"They didn't like that ... They were a kindly lot really. They tried tossing half the cargo into the sea to steady the ship. But it didn't work.

"So in the end, the captain said he was very sorry,
and they threw me over the side too."

"That sounds like the end of the story," said Dan.

"You might well think so," said Jonah, "... and I must say, I thought my last hour had come. I was freezing cold and half full of salt water, *and* I couldn't swim.

"I was about to go under for the last time, when suddenly up came an enormous fish. What kind of fish, I don't know, but it was huge! I hardly had time to look at it before it opened its great mouth and swallowed me whole."

"Just like the worm," said Rachel.

"Just like the worm ... but at least I was safe from the sea."

"What about the ship?" asked Dan.

"That was safe too. Later I heard that the storm died down and they got to land safely.

"But believe me, it wasn't much fun inside that fish. Three whole days and nights I was in its belly. I marked up each day on one of the ribs.

"It got hotter and smellier and more and more uncomfortable. And every time the fish had a tummy rumble, it sounded like a thunderstorm!"

"So what did you do?" asked Dan.

"Prayed to God, that's what I did. Said I was sorry. Praying's the best thing you can do when you're in real trouble.

"And believe it or not, God heard me, all that way from the bottom of the sea ... because the next thing I knew, the fish opened its mouth and spat me out on to dry land."

"Because God told it to?" asked Rachel.

"The fish probably had a tummy-ache," said Dan.

"Maybe both," said his uncle, "but I'd hardly had time to see where I was when God started talking to me again.

" 'Oh, no,' I thought. 'What now?'

" 'Up you get, Jonah,' he said. 'Go to Nineveh, and tell the people that if they don't mend their ways, I, God, shall destroy them all, and their city too.'

"Well, I seemed to have heard that before somewhere; only this time I knew better than to run away. I ran all the way *to* Nineveh instead!

"And I got up in the marketplace and told everyone just what God had said. And they believed me—everyone from the king down. They did away with all their rich clothes and put on sackcloth instead. And they stopped eating—to show they really meant to mend their ways."

"So then what?" asked Dan. "Did God let them off, after all?"

"Yes, he did—worse luck," answered Jonah. "I went away and sat down outside the walls, to see what would happen. I watched and I waited, but nothing did happen.

"I was furious, I can tell you. Although I'd done what God said, I really wanted to see God put an end to Nineveh and all its horrible people.

"I was angry and hot sitting there in the blazing sun. Then God grew a special leafy plant to give me shade.

"That was good, but the next day he let it wither away. I got sick and tired of the whole business.

"I said, 'Listen, God, I'm wasting my time sitting around here. I might just as well be dead!'

"But God said, 'Jonah, stop fussing about yourself and what *you* think all the time! I have many more places and things and people to care for than just you. And that includes everybody in Nineveh.'

"Then at last I understood. God loves us *all*. He wants to see us well and happy and being good. He cares very much for everything he has made: people, cities, ships, plants, birds and beasts, fishes large and small..."

"And even worms?" asked
Rachel.

"Even worms!" said Jonah.